D0114570

© 2003 by Barbour Publishing, Inc.

ISBN 1-59310-224-0

Cover design by Julie Doll

Scripture quotations are taken from the HOLY BIBLE, NEW INTERNATIONAL VERSION®. NIV®. Copyright © 1973, 1978, 1984 by International Bible Society. Used by permission of Zondervan Publishing House. All rights reserved.

Definitions are taken from *Merriam-Webster's Collegiate Dictionary*.

Published by Humble Creek, P.O. Box 719, Uhrichsville, Ohio 44683

Printed in China.
5 4 3 2 1

Everyday Love

KELLY WILLIAMS

HUMBLECREEK
INSPIRATION FOR LIFE

If I speak in the tongues of men and of angels, but have not love, I am only a resounding gong or a clanging cymbal. If I have the gift of prophecy and can fathom all mysteries and all knowledge, and if I have a faith that can move mountains, but have not love, I am nothing. If I give all I possess to the poor and surrender my body to the flames, but have not love, I gain nothing. Love is patient, love is kind. It does not envy, it does not boast, it is not proud. It is not rude, it is not self-seeking, it is not easily angered, it keeps no record of wrongs. Love does not delight in evil but rejoices with the truth. It always protects, always trusts, always hopes, always perseveres. Love never fails.

1 CORINTHIANS 13:1–8

Everyday Love

what is it?

everyday adj. 1. encountered or used routinely or
typically

love n. 1. strong affection for another arising out of
kinship or personal ties 2. warm attachment,
enthusiasm, or devotion 3. unselfish loyal and
benevolent concern for the good of another

Put those words together,
and you get something pretty special—
a love that happens every day
of the year! . . .

Everyday love offers everything but the ordinary.

❤ ❤ ❤

Everyday Love

. . .is unconditional.

. . .offers comfort and acceptance.

. . .is giving.

. . .is unfailing and never ending.

. . .creates beauty in the most unexpected places.

Love is the master key
that opens the gates
of happiness.

OLIVER WENDELL HOLMES

❤❤❤

MY bounty is as boundless as the sea,
My love as deep;
The more I give to thee
The more I have,
For both are infinite.

WILLIAM SHAKESPEARE

♥♥♥

Love is

something eternal....

Vincent van Gogh

♥♥♥

Love feels no burden, thinks nothing of trouble,
attempts what is above its strength,
pleads no excuse of impossibility.
It is therefore able to undertake all things,
and it completes many things, and warrants them to take effect,
where he who does not love would faint and lie down.
Love is watchful and sleeping, slumbereth not.
Though weary, it is not tired;
though pressed, it is not straitened;
though alarmed, it is not confounded.

THOMAS À KEMPIS

❤❤❤

Ella was tired and frustrated. Her husband worked long hours—sometimes away for days at a time on a construction site out of town. Her own job demanded extra-long hours and offered little appreciation in return. It took everything she had just to get out of bed in the mornings. Ella needed a break.

Feeling more worn out than usual one Tuesday morning, she walked into her office at work and saw she had a voice mail message. *Now what?* she thought. *Any message this early in the morning can't be good.* She punched in her access code and listened. . . .

"Hi, honey. I miss you. Just wanted to tell you that I hope you have a good day. I'll see you tonight. I love you."

Joy filled her heart as she played the message once more. A simple act of everyday love had brightened Ella's dreary Tuesday morning. She sat down at her desk with a smile on her face, ready to start a new day.

❤❤❤

Love comforteth
like sunshine
after rain.

WILLIAM SHAKESPEARE

We are not the same persons this year as last;
nor are those we love.
It is a happy chance if we, changing,
continue to love a changed person.

W. SOMERSET MAUGHAM

❤❤❤

The greatest happiness of life is
the conviction that we are loved—
loved for ourselves, or rather, loved in spite of ourselves.

VICTOR HUGO

You will find as you look back upon your life
that the moments when you have truly lived
are the moments when you have done things in the spirit of love.

HENRY DRUMMOND

*Carve your name on hearts
and not on marble.*

CHARLES H. SPURGEON

♥♥♥

Love is
the river of life
in the world.

HENRY WARD BEECHER

♥♥♥

Dear Heavenly Father,

May the love that shines from my heart be
an example to others, as I want them to see You through me.
Help me to use my love every day in small ways;
for it's often the simple acts of love that hold
the most profound meaning and have the greatest effects
upon hearts. Amen.

Generally, by the time you are Real, most of your hair has been loved off, and your eyes drop out and you get loose in the joints and very shabby. But these things don't matter at all, because once you are Real you can't be ugly, except to people who don't understand.

MARGERY WILLIAMS,
The Velveteen Rabbit

Jake had a favorite stuffed teddy bear that was given to him at birth. Through the years the cuddly bear had seen more than his share of kisses, hugs, tugs, and squeezes. He had traveled more than all of Jake's other stuffed animals. His fluffy brown fur was wearing off in patches, he had no left eye, and his arms and legs hung by a few stitches of loose thread.

With each birthday and Christmas, as Jake grew up, he received numerous "new" stuffed friends, but they were quickly forgotten and set aside for his best-loved, tattered bear. Numerous times Jake's parents tried to get rid of the bear. . .but Jake refused to part with his friend, who gave him comfort beyond what any new toy could offer. There could be no replacement.

Jake's everyday love for his bear was unconditional. To him this ragged bear was more beautiful than any new toy he could possibly receive.

❤ ❤ ❤

Older now, Jake has far outgrown his childhood toys. But he has a stuffed bear named Scooby, who is living out his days in Jake's closet (placed safely on a shelf where he won't acquire any more "stress" on his weary joints).

Love is
a great beautifier.

LOUISA MAY ALCOTT

The consciousness of loving and being loved
brings a warmth and a richness to life
that nothing else can bring.

OSCAR WILDE

♥♥♥

*Love is
the only gold.*

ALFRED, LORD TENNYSON

Spread love everywhere you go: first of all in your own house. Give love to your children, to your wife or husband, to a next door neighbor. . . . Let no one ever come to you without leaving better and happier. Be the living expression of God's kindness; kindness in your face, kindness in your eyes, kindness in your smile, kindness in your warm greeting.

MOTHER TERESA

To love is to place our happiness in the happiness of another.

GOTTFRIED WILHELM VON LEIBNIZ

May the Lord make your love increase
and overflow for each other.

1 THESSALONIANS 3:12

❤❤❤

Shelly's sister-in-law, Jean, had experienced a particularly rough year full of emotional turmoil. Jean withdrew from activities, seeming depressed and unhappy with her life.

A few months prior to a holiday get-together, though, Jean experienced some life-altering events—she found a new job and met her wonderful husband-to-be. Shelly began to see an incredible transformation take place. Jean smiled more. Her eyes were full of life and an excitement that Shelly had never seen.

On Thanksgiving Day, as the family relaxed in the living room discussing their blessings, Shelly spoke up. "Jean, I am most thankful for your happiness. I've never seen you so content and happy. You're a new person."

Jean only smiled—but her expression spoke volumes. No one had ever expressed such concern for her own happiness. This simple act of everyday love is one that Jean would remember for years to come.

❤❤❤

I love you not only for what you are,
but for what I am when I am with you.
I love you not only for what you have made of yourself,
but for what you are making of me.
I love you for the part of me that you bring out.

ELIZABETH BARRETT BROWNING

We are shaped and fashioned
by what we love.

JOHANN WOLFGANG VON GOETHE

Dear friends,

let us love one another,

for love comes from God.

1 JOHN 4:7

The best and most beautiful things
cannot be seen or even touched.
They must be felt with the heart.

HELEN KELLER

♥♥♥

This is the miracle that happens every time
to those who really love; the more they give,
the more they possess of that precious nourishing love
from which flowers and children have their strength.

RAINER MARIA RILKE

Love is something like the clouds that were in the sky before the sun came out. . . . You cannot touch the clouds, you know; but you feel the rain and know how glad the flowers are to have it after a hot day. You cannot touch love either; but you feel the sweetness that it pours into everything. Without love you would not be happy. . . .

ANNIE SULLIVAN

Some people come into our lives,
leave footprints on our hearts,
and we are never the same.

AUTHOR UNKNOWN

"As the Father has loved me,
so have I loved you."

JOHN 15:9

You learn to speak by speaking, to study by studying,
to run by running, to work by working;
in just the same way, you learn to love by loving.

St. Francis de Sales

❤❤❤

When the heart speaks, however simple the words,
its language is always acceptable to those who have hearts.

Mary Baker Eddy

Love one another.

JOHN 13:34

♥♥♥

We can do no great things;

only small things

with great love.

MOTHER TERESA

Everyday Love

Everyday love can be expressed in little ways. . .

- Send a "thinking of you" card to someone who's had a trying week.

- Call a friend across the country just to say "hi."

- Offer your free babysitting services to young parents in need of a night out.

- Spend time with a child—playing, reading, cuddling. . .

- Send flowers to a loved one—just because.

- Visit a lonely neighbor.

- Volunteer your free time for a good cause—pet shelter, literacy program, hospital, church, soup kitchen. . .

- Pray with a friend who has a special need.

Keep love in your heart.

OSCAR WILDE

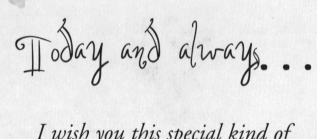

Today and always. . .

I wish you this special kind of
"everyday love"
in your heart.